READ IF YOU'RE HEARTBROKEN

Angeline Lowther

BookLeaf Publishing

India | USA | UK

Presentation by *BookLeaf Publishing*

Web: www.bookleafpub.com

E-mail: info@bookleafpub.com

ISBN: 9789358313253

First edition 2023

DEDICATION

Joshua Allan Gage..

I loved you then, I love you still.

I always have and I always will.

Unconditional Love

Is it too much to say I miss you,
even though you were never mine?

Is it okay to be so blue,
when stars didn't quite align?

How is it still I think of you,
when times are both happy and tough?

My only answer is, in fact,
I could never love you enough.

Voyage Of A Broken Heart

2

Hellish is the raging sea that pulsates deep inside
me,
Hardly able to steer the ship as the waves crash
all around me,
The strength it takes to fill a life that forever
feels so lonely,
Is the meaning of death in life itself, where
depression feels so homely.

Unrequited

A fire burns deep inside me that brings calm to
all my senses,
the passion is the burning light that tears through
all my defences.

The eyes in which you look at me brings calm to
the raging storm,
and while the fire hurts sometimes, it keeps me
safe and warm.

It's elegant to our see souls dance as they
intertwine,
and while your soul feels little spark, I feel it
deep in mine.

This curse which lays upon me has been shaken
but never broken,
the antidote lives only in three words you've
never spoken.

Dark Thoughts

Life isn't fair,

Life is cruel.

Life isn't sunshine,

Life is darkness.

Life isn't exciting,

Life is exhausting.

Life isn't easy,

Life is pain.

Fuck Narcissists

"I love you", he said,
"No you don't", she said
All the things you said,
Still stuck in my head.

All the nights of crying,
All the tears alone,
Caught in the crossfire,
Lord please take me home.

"I lied", he said
"Yes you did", she said
All the things you did,
So shallow and morbid.

All the fighting and swearing,
All the "I'm done" and "you're blocked",
Those loving memories,
Sealed shut and all locked.

Cry For Help

It doesn't matter how much time I spend with
him,
I can't feel the same things I felt with you.

If you knew how badly he treated me,
It would shock you too.

He's fun and makes me laugh,
But he plays games and it hurts.

The lies and secrets shatter me,
Through the ego and evils he exerts.

But I don't have you, so I need him,
Emotionally damaged and needing human touch.

I don't know how far you are, and I know you
can't hear me,
But I want you to know that I need you so much.

His infidelity

You know the night we kissed?
We were all alone.

It was the feeling my soul missed,
Through many lifetimes ago.

You are the deepest yearn of my heart,
My life's biggest high.

This life has kept us so far apart,
Like we aren't meant to be.

But if that's the reason we aren't one,
Why did you feel the connection?

Even though all is said and done,
Why do I dream of you?

Those soft brown eyes and kissable lips,
The passion never faded.

When you pulled me close, hands on hips,
Did you think of her?

The ignition between us lit so strong,
Why do you have to be married?

My morals and my ethics knew it was wrong,
But we both knew we were falling.

Now all I have is memories of us,
And what we could have been.

You had to go back and win her trust,
Leaving me without my best friend.

I Haiku'd About You

Life is scaring me.
Where are you when I need you.
I need your old soul.

You're Not In Love With Her

It was an old pub over north where we met,
I asked someone who you were.
It's a night of my life I'll never forget,
Although some of it kind of a blur.
We had a crazy connection from the start,
And you were the first to admit it.
It wasn't long until you captured my heart,
My soul feeling yours bit by bit.
I fell in love so quickly,
But you made sure you held back,
Losing you made me sickly,
And I came under attack.
While I wish you both a happy life,
It should have been me who you called wife.

The Other Heartbreak

Lies as old as a fossil,
Stories as tall as a hill.
The evil within you colossal,
And your eyes that haunt me still.
Why do you think I'm a fool,
When I'm always a step ahead.
Drowning in depths of the tear pool,
Suffocating from months of dread.
I never fell in love,
But I could have if you tried.
The good times fit like a glove,
With your smile dripped in pride.
I wish you could really love me,
I wish we were meant to be.

I Think I'm Falling For You

If you would please,
I would like your time.

Just a spare moment,
With your hand in mine.

It doesn't need to be public,
It doesn't need to be known,

All I want is this moment,
With you, and you alone.

We've been seeing each other a while,
And I like your company.

So is it ok if we just..
Slip into eternity?

Give Me A Chance

All that you are,
All that you've done,
And if only I was the one.

Who would hold your hand,
Who would calm your fears,
And stay with you through all the years.

I'd be the sun,
To your moon,
Please don't leave me quite so soon.

I have so much to offer,
So much to show,
I'm begging you baby..don't let me go.

The Calm To Your Storm

What are your nightmares about?
Can you share them with me?
You cry and you shout,
Your mind won't let you be.

You're tossing and turning,
And it breaks me to see,
It's like you are burning,
Come back to me.

You finally wake,
My hand on your cheek,
The moonlight opaque,
My eyes you so seek.

I hope you know,
I'm always here,
I'll never let you go,
I won't disappear.

Your Yin And Yang

Typical, logical,
Egotistical, mechanical.

Lyrical, magical,
whimsical, angelical.

Depression Two Point Oh

Darkness surrounds the chambers of the ocean
floor,
The ship has sunk and I can't see anymore,
Rocking and swaying with the loss of gravity,
Among Mother Nature and her deep-seeded
vanity.

I cry out for help but no one can hear me,
Losing my breath and what's left of my sanity,
Is it the end,
Or is it just the beginning,
Will I drown again?
Or start over swimming?

Let Him Go

He doesn't want you,
He doesn't care,
He doesn't love you,
He's never there.

The lies he tells you,
The webs he spins,
The tales that haunt you,
He always wins.

Pain he causes,
Pain he creates,
Pain he uses,
Pain he makes.

Let go of him,
Let go of it all,
Let go of the bond,
Or else you'll fall.

Make-Up Sex

The devil is so handsome,
My heart is the ransom,
The burning fires of hell,
I'm under your spell.

The flashes of pain,
Come and go again,
The award of rekindling,
And sexy thoughts lingering.

The forbidden human touch,
My body in your clutch,
Holding me tight,
Until I feel cascading delight.

Goodbye Red Flags

Your flag is red,
Mine is white,
Left by myself,
Alone at night.

I'm glad you're gone,
But better still,
I'll love myself,
And I always will.